You
GE

—— Leroy Mervan ——

CONTENTS

Pages 2-3
and 34-35:
Photos by
Michael Gilroy

© 1991
By T.F.H.
Publications,
Inc., Neptune,
N.J. 07753 USA

——— • ———

T.F.H.
Publications,
The Spinney,
Parklands,
Denmead,
Portsmouth
PO7 6AR
England

Introduction

As pets, gerbils are relatively new. For this reason you may be called upon frequently to answer the question, "What's a gerbil?"

With luck, you may find *gerbil* listed in your dictionary or encyclopedia. The word is pronounced *jur-bil* and comes from the Latin *gerbillus,* meaning "little jerboa." Probably your reference book will briefly define the gerbil as a "jerboa-like animal." Looking up jerboa, you may learn that this is a jumping desert rodent found in Asia and Africa. But this isn't much help, since neither the gerbil nor the jerboa is a native of the Western Hemisphere.

GERBILS IN THE WILD

Gerbils are the typical small mammals found in remote arid regions of Asia, Africa, and Eastern Europe. They are similar to jumping rodents such as jerboas and kangaroo rats, but their size, body extremities, and jumping motions are not so exaggerated. They are said to be one of the most graceful small rodents in their movements.

Little is known of the gerbil's life in the wild, where they are called desert rats, sand rats, or jirds. Like hamsters, they are burrowing animals which live far from sources of water. They eat seeds, grains, grasses, roots, and plants found in their desert environment.

Apparently gerbils are active during the day and to some extent at night. They live in colonies and have some close social contact. Their home is a tunnel, six to eight feet long. It has several entrances, extends several feet underground, and usually has branch tunnels at different levels. Various chambers along the main tunnel serve as rooms for nesting and food storage.

MONGOLIAN GERBILS

Recent references place gerbils in the family Cricetidae, to which hamsters belong. All true gerbils belong to a subfamily Gerbillinae, which consists of about ten genera and a total of some 40 species which differ only slightly in size and appearance.

The species most readily available today is the Mongolian gerbil, originating in northeastern China and eastern Mongolia. Throughout this book the word "gerbil" will be understood to mean "Mongolian gerbil."

In the family tree of animals, pet gerbils are members of the order Rodentia, suborder Myomorpha, super-family Muroidea, family Cricetidae, subfamily Gerbillinae, genus *Meriones,* and species *unguiculatus.* Thus, the scientific name *Meriones unguiculatus* is used to denote Mongolian gerbils.

Meriones was a Greek warrior who boasted a helmet decorated with boars' tusks; *unguiculatus* comes from a Latin word meaning "fingernail." This "tooth-and-nail" concept seems very inappropriate for such a small, amiable animal!

Mature gerbils are smaller than rats but larger than mice. They are about four inches long, with a furry tufted tail of about the same length. Their weight seldom exceeds four ounces.

The fur on their back and tail is a tawny or reddish brown, with black outer tips and a gray undercoat. The underside of the body is light gray or creamy white. The head is broader and more foreshortened, with less prominent ears than that of the rat or mouse. The eyes are large, dark, and bulge slightly. The hind legs are elongated and the forefeet are relatively small; each foot has five toes with long, thin nails.

Thus, the gerbil has evolved with a protective desert coloration and with limbs adapted for standing, leaping, burrowing, sitting, scurrying, or hopping. Their general coloring, appearance, postures, and actions are similar to those of some squirrels and chipmunks.

GERBILS IN RESEARCH

Gerbils were introduced to the United States by Dr. Victor Schwentker in 1954. Since that time there has been a growing scientific interest in these animals because of their unique characteristics and susceptibilities, plus their ease of care, gentle disposition, and other factors.

The gerbil can live normally with very little drinking water; this fact may be of importance in man's future space travels. The gerbil's heat tolerance and body temperature regulation are superior to those found in most other desert animals. When fed a fat-rich diet, they adjust easily to high cholesterol levels, which are linked to heart and blood vessel ailments in humans.

Additionally, gerbils have a relatively high resistance to radiation exposure. They possess an unusual abdominal gland that could be useful in studying human hormone actions. Some experiments have shown that gerbils may be of importance in cancer research. Studies involving blood composition, body cells, parasitic diseases, and virus infections may also prove significant.

In psychology and in behavioral research, gerbils are superior to white rats in some tests, and their docile nature has led to their use in treating some emotionally disturbed children.

GERBILS AS PETS

After earning the name "gentle gerbils" in the laboratory, it was almost inevitable that these animals should enter the pet world. By 1965, through TV appearances, press articles, classroom interest, and word-of-mouth, gerbils became well established as very desirable pets.

These are not "cuddly" pets, but they seem to enjoy being handled and will not bite unless they're mistreated. Their friendliness, curiosity, pert expressions, and quick, squirrel-like movements are fascinating to adults and children alike.

Gerbils have simple requirements for housing, food, and water. They can be left unattended for days if food and water are available. They are clean, odorless, and easy to keep that way. They are healthy and hardy. They make very little noise.

Climate is no problem if temperature can be maintained within reasonable limits. There is no hibernation in winter nor stupor in summer, and gerbils are active during the daytime. They have little tendency to escape and are relatively easy to recapture if they should get loose.

Because gerbils seem happiest and most active when kept in mated pairs, the question of what to do with their offspring must be considered. An alternative might be to obtain a pair of gerbils beyond breeding age which still can provide you with plenty of interesting activity and friendly behavior.

The gerbil's overall attributes indicate that it can be a suitable pet in virtually any type of home—city, farm, or suburban dwelling.

The ideal house for a gerbil will be lightweight, durable, and easy to maintain. Photo courtesy Rolf C. Hagen Corp.

A stunning array of gerbil houses and specially manufactured accommodations is available from pet shops and pet-supply dealers. This smart gerbil is busily inspecting its new home. Photo by Michael Gilroy.

Behavior

The gerbil has several specific habits and customs which are interesting to observe. These are a part of the animal's daily life and worthy of some knowledge by the pet owner so that he will understand his pets better. Certain behavior is not well understood and further study is needed to gain new knowledge about gerbils.

ACTIVITY CYCLE

The gerbil's life is one of cyclic activity. He alternates periods of intense activity with short periods of sleep or rest throughout the day. When awake, he darts to and fro like a chipmunk. He curiously investigates every new occurrence. He nibbles at food continually to support his bursts of energy. He burrows into his bedding, gnaws on available material, and makes nests. His intense participation in these activities makes it easy to understand why he needs occasional rest!

A gerbil often stretches out his forefeet and yawns almost like a cat or a dog. As you might guess, a nap soon follows. Sleep can be deep and uninterrupted; except for his breathing, you may wonder sometimes whether he is still alive. In warm weather, he may rearrange the bedding to lie on the bare cage floor. He'll curl up on his side, stretch out on his stomach, or even lie flat on his back! In cool weather, gerbils often sleep close together or on top of each other. They like to tuck their head down between their hind feet and curl their tail around their body— thus resembling a two-inch "ball of fluff."

During the gerbil's periods of rest or sleep, the pet owner should not disturb the animal. This would be contrary to the gerbil's natural way of life, and he might become irritable— like a child who misses his nap.

CURIOSITY

This trait dominates the gerbil's active behavior to a considerable extent. When you approach the gerbils' cage, they will invariably come to the nearest side to see what new food or plaything you have for them to try out. They're eager to inspect or investigate almost any toy or object offered to them: tubes, toy bridges or ladders, vehicles, baskets, carts, boxes, empty cans, pieces of cloth or paper, building blocks, etc. (Because of the gerbil's gnawing habits, be sure that these objects cannot harm the animals.) His interest is short-lived with one toy or new object, and curiosity makes him ready to explore a new one soon.

This curiosity drive is so great that a hungry gerbil subjected to a maze test with food at its end will stop to explore each "dead end" passage in the maze before he reaches the end!

If you stick your hand into his cage, the gerbil's first reaction is to sniff it and examine it further. Usually, he'll want to climb your hand and arm for more exploring, if you are willing.

Fearlessness is closely related to curiosity at times. In captivity, the gerbil has little chance to learn fear from his experience or his parents' experience. Sudden movements or noises may startle gerbils, especially the young ones, but this reaction seems to be one of surprise more than fear. Generally, no fear is apparent in their exposure to strange objects, people, noises, lights, or other pets. Because of this lack of fear, you should be cautious in allowing your gerbils to come into contact with other animals. Some dogs and cats can be trained to tolerate gerbils, but others may regard the gerbil as a tasty meal or a handy plaything to tease.

BURROWING

Burrowing and scratching are normal activities for gerbils. In the wild, they spend much time burrowing to make their homes and to search for food among the desert scrub and grass. Their short forefeet make rapid digging motions, and the hind legs kick the excavated material to the rear—much like the lawn-digging actions of a dog. Sometimes the head is also used to push material or objects out of the way.

The sharp nails on the gerbil's forefeet can eventually burrow through cardboard or make scratches in wood or plastic. However, the author does not know of an instance where a pet owner has been scratched enough to break the skin.

On occasion you may look into the gerbil cage and think that you have lost a pet. Chances are that the "missing" animal has burrowed completely beneath the bedding material. Rap lightly on the cage and you'll probably see a cute, whiskered face pop up, like a miniature squirrel emerging from a pile of leaves!

GNAWING

The gerbil's incisors grow throughout his lifetime. If they're too long or too short, he could not survive for long. In captivity this is seldom a problem—if necessary you can provide a block of wood for tooth exercise, although the hard food in the diet usually suffices.

At one time or another, gerbils will attempt to gnaw or chew on almost any available material—bedding, nest material, paper, cardboard, cloth, wood, bone, plastic, and even metal. This is a normal part of their everyday life.

LOCOMOTION

The ability to jump with his hind limbs is a characteristic that makes the gerbil a unique pet and has earned him the nickname "pocket kangaroo." In the wild, gerbils can jump several feet if need be. Young gerbils can use their hind legs for jumping by the time they're weaned.

Ladders and other similar devices make the gerbil's habitat interesting for your pet. This cinnamon gerbil spends much of its active time climbing. Photo by Michael Gilroy.

This young lady is sure to steal the heart of any new gerbil fan. Standing on hind legs this gerbil demonstrates good balance. The gerbil's tail is an important component in the animal's balancing act. Photo by Michael Gilroy.

When a cage full of youngsters is suddenly startled, it looks like a box of jumping beans scattering in various directions! Older gerbils will not jump so frequently, although they still have the ability. In captivity, even unconfined gerbils seldom jump more than about 18 inches horizontally or 6 inches vertically.

Some gerbils hop straight up when startled. They can jump forward, backward, sideways, or even turn completely around in mid-air if they desire.

Usually, gerbils move about on all four feet, with their short forefeet providing limited balance and support. From time to time, they pause to sit or stand on their hind legs—like squirrels. This is their preferred eating or drinking position. To satisfy their curiosity, gerbils will stand erect, stretch upward, and even lean backward slightly—while still maintaining their balance.

The tail is used to good advantage. It gives the gerbil balance while sitting, standing, or landing after a leap. During a jump, it may act like a rudder to help guide the animal through the air.

Gerbils can climb wire mesh vertically with no difficulty, but they cannot hang upside-down from a mesh cage roof for long.

NOISES

These pets are relatively quiet animals. Their only vocal sound is a faint, high-pitched *chee-chee,* more like the cheeping of a bird than the squeaking of a rodent. Even this sound is infrequent, unless a litter of young is present or the parents have a brief "family argument."

From weaning age, most gerbils can make a sound on the cage bedding or floor by rapidly drumming or thumping their hind legs. This staccato *ta-ta-tat* may be a warning signal, like the slapping of a beaver's tail. It seems to signify *Attention!* and may be repeated by other gerbils within hearing. It also seems to indicate excitement in new surroundings or at mating time.

The rapid burrowing or scratching action of the forefeet against the cage floor or walls also produces a characteristic rustling or rasping sound.

GROOMING

Gerbils like to be clean, and they keep themselves well groomed with little effort on your part.

Using forepaws and tongue, they "scrub" their face, head, ears, body, and tail in cat-like fashion. One gerbil will often groom another. These actions promote cleanliness, stimulate the skin, prevent matting of the fur, and help keep the coat glossy.

Because gerbils come from very dry climates, their skin produces certain natural oils to combat dryness. Dampness or high humidity may counteract the purpose of these oils and result in a ruffled coat, which the animals take care of by grooming and by rolling in dry bedding material.

Selecting

By the age of one month, the odds are that a gerbil will lead a full and healthy life; add a few weeks to this age just to increase your odds, and get your gerbils when they're about six to eight weeks old. At this age they will be fairly rugged, not too nervous, and their appearance and actions will afford you much pleasure.

Gerbils are most active and seem to be happiest when kept in sexed pairs. Two mature males or females may fight if kept together, especially if they were raised in different families. The same is true for mixed groups of older males and females.

If you must keep a single gerbil, either sex seems to be equally satisfactory. Be sure to give sufficient attention and provide playthings to keep your pet active and contented.

APPEARANCE

Look for those animals whose movements and actions are quick and bobbing, like a squirrel or a chipmunk. They should be alert—an unexpected movement on your part should startle them.

The body should be moderately filled out and firm-looking; a too fat appearance may be due to old age or overfeeding. The fur should be relatively long, soft, and glossy, like that of a flying squirrel. The amount and distribution of black hair among the reddish brown vary. The underside should be light gray or creamy white.

The nose and head should be somewhat foreshortened rather than long and thin. The ears should be fairly small, not too rounded, and should stand erect. The eyes should be fairly large (but not bulge excessively), dark, and twinkling or bright in appearance.

Some variations occur in tail length and thickness, but in choosing young gerbils this is purely guesswork, as the tail is only one-fourth as long as the gerbil's body at birth and almost the same length as the body when the animal is full-grown.

A kink in the tail or a stubby tail with a blunt tip—even though tufted—may be the result of injury.

Fighting may produce a partly closed eye, a scab on the mouth, a lump on the head or nose, or sore spots on the rump. Be sure to examine the feet and nails to see that they are in good condition.

Bald spots could mean a dietary deficiency. Frequent scratching of the fur may indicate the presence of external parasites.

Runny eyes or nose, a wet bottom, skin ulcerations, unusual lumps, or sores may signal a disease or a condition that could be beyond your care.

Many rodents are known for their agouti coloration. On the gerbil, the agouti color is most attractive—note the different shades of each hair on the coat of this handsome specimen. Photo by Michael Gilroy.

An agouti gerbil accompanied by an equally appealing cinnamon gerbil. While color may influence your selection, be sure to take note of the animal's vital signs first. Photo by Michael Gilroy.

Housing

Pet shops offer a variety of cages that are suitable for housing gerbils. Cages can be made of wood, sheet metal, glass, plastic, wire mesh or grid, or combinations of these materials.

CAGES

Gerbils seem to fare best in cages with solid bottoms. A floor space about 10 by 20 inches or 15 by 15 inches is adequate for a pair plus a litter of offspring. The standard "large" hamster cage, "small animal" cage, ten-gallon aquarium, and even some large bird cages sold in pet shops may meet these requirements.

To allow for the gerbil's habit of eating or drinking from a sitting position, plus some "stretching" space, an overall cage height of eight to ten inches is desirable.

Each type of cage has advantages or disadvantages in durability, sanitation, weight, and security. Metal, plastic, and glass are preferred for ease of cleaning. Wood is least expensive but also the least durable and sanitary. (Gerbils can and will gnaw exposed wood surfaces, unless flush, and they can scratch wood and plastic surfaces to some extent.)

Normally your gerbils will not jump high enough to escape from an aquarium or open-top cage, but it's best to provide some form of top or lid to keep out "intruders" and still allow ventilation. These covers can be made of wire mesh or be purchased in standard sizes from your pet dealer.

The spacing of the cage wire mesh or grid should be one-half inch or less; this will prevent sore spots from forming on the gerbil's nose during his attempts to gnaw the metal. Insect screening should not be used within the animals' reach, as they might scratch or gnaw through it.

It is preferable that the cage sides and ends be solid to a height of several inches above the floor to reduce the scattering of the bedding material (which may result from the animals' burrowing). This may also prevent the accidental loss of newborn gerbils through the mesh or grid openings, and it provides protection against drafts.

BEDDING

Bedding material should be provided on the cage floor to a depth of two or three inches. The gerbils will arrange it to suit their needs, depending on the temperature and their own desires.

This material should be clean, absorbent, dustless, and non-toxic. Pine shavings, coarse sawdust, excelsior, crushed corncobs, husks, grass, leaves, or any commercial "litter" material will be adequate.

CLEANLINESS

Gerbils are perhaps the cleanest of all pet animals. Their body wastes amount to so little that the cage bedding material needs changing only every two or three weeks! And if a litter of young arrives at normal cage-cleaning time, you can wait until weaning time to change the bedding. Of course you should change the bedding if it becomes soaked due to spilled water or if it is obviously soiled. Bedding may have to be changed more frequently in warm weather than during cool weather.

Routine cage cleaning consists of a brief scraping and sweeping of the cage when the soiled bedding is removed. Several times a year you should use a household disinfectant solution to clean the cage and utensils. Be sure to dry and air the cage thoroughly before returning the animals.

When your gerbils are put back in their cage after the bedding is renewed, they will burrow into it and work industriously to rearrange it. This is a good time to put a small piece of soft cloth in the cage for the gerbils to shred into nesting material, which will last until the next bedding change.

FURNISHINGS

If sufficient floor space is provided, gerbils are not afflicted with any kind of "paralysis." Even so, most gerbils will enjoy using an exercise wheel, which provides a good outlet for their excess energy.

A food container, a standard watering bottle, some toys or playthings, and a piece of wood for gnawing will complete the "furnishings" of the gerbils' home.

TEMPERATURE AND HUMIDITY

In his native environment, the gerbil can stay comfortable by retreating to his burrow during the heat of the day or the chill of the night, when necessary. In captivity his requirements are nearly the same as those of your home—about 70 to 80°F and 40 to 60 percent relative humidity. Temperatures as low as 50°F can be tolerated if sufficient bedding and nesting material are provided.

If your climate permits, gerbil cages can be located outdoors, assuming that you provide adequate protection against rain, sun, wind, and predators.

Gerbils kept in an aquarium or in transparent plastic cages must be protected from exposure to direct sunlight. The sun's rays, plus the insulating and possibly magnifying properties of the cage walls, might raise the inside temperature above 100°F, *which could be fatal!*

The cage can be kept in a basement, garage, or spare room, as desired. Because of the gerbil's cleanliness and lack of odor, there is usually no reason to prevent you from keeping them in almost any room of your house.

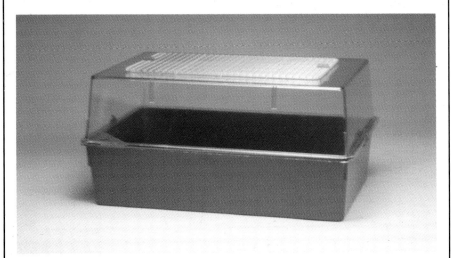

Above: You can choose from a wide variety of attractive cages for your gerbil. Below: Whatever kind of bedding that you choose, be sure to change it on a regular basis to prevent the buildup of harmful bacteria. Photos courtesy Rolf C. Hagen Corp.

Always be wary of the plants and flowers with which your gerbil has contact. Some plants are poisonous and should be kept out of the gerbil's path. Photo by Michael Gilroy.

ESCAPES

The burrowing, scratching, and gnawing activities of gerbils do not necessarily mean that they're anxious to escape. These actions form an instinctive part of their daily life. Probably you'll suffer one or more accidental escapes of your pet gerbils, so let's discuss methods of recapture.

Often an escaped gerbil shows a willingness to return to his cage voluntarily if it is in sight. You may be able to speed up his return by putting some sunflower seeds near the cage. And if you remain still, he may wander back to your vicinity after he explores his immediate surroundings.

Because gerbils love to explore tunnels, one successful means of recapture is to place a cardboard or plastic tube near an escaped gerbil (use some seeds or bedding as bait if necessary). When he enters the tube, cup your hands over the ends, pick up the tube, and return the gerbil to his cage. Or you can use a baited coffee can or other empty container on its side and pick it up once the gerbil is inside.

You can also employ the trick used in recapturing hamsters. Place a bucket in the room where your gerbil escaped and make the room escape-proof. Make a series of "steps" from the floor up to the bucket lip, using wood blocks or bricks. Put some seeds and bedding on the steps and in the bucket; you can also put the escaped animal's mate inside the bucket (ensure that the bucket is high enough that the animals can't jump out). By the next morning your escaped gerbil should be safely in the bucket.

Most gerbils recognize their cage and will return back to it voluntarily.

Diet

To maintain your pet's health and to meet his energy needs, you must provide a balanced diet that will meet all of the requirements for good gerbil nutrition.

DRY FOOD

Pelletized gerbil food, available at pet shops, is specially formulated to satisfy the dietary requirements of gerbils. It contains assortments of grains such as wheat, corn, oats, and barley, as well as sunflower seeds, pumpkin seeds (and other small seeds), peanuts, and vegetable flakes. This special gerbil food should form the bulk of your pet's diet.

Some hobbyists occasionally offer their gerbils potato chips, shelled peanuts, pretzel sticks, crackers, and similar snacks.

How much food to give is easily learned through experience. Generally, about a tablespoonful per day per adult, and about half that for a young animal, should be enough.

There is no rule as to the time (of day) for feeding. Daily, in the late afternoon, is perhaps most convenient. Your gerbils will learn to anticipate feeding time and will become very active on hearing the sounds associated with their feeding routine. They do not hoard food and—except for sunflower seeds— they will not overeat.

SUNFLOWER SEEDS

Sunflower seeds are the gerbil's favorite treat. It is fascinating to watch a gerbil deftly hold and manipulate a seed in his forepaws, slit the shell with his sharp incisors, extract and devour the meat, then discard the husk and reach for another. This neat trick is mastered by most gerbils by age three weeks. These seeds should *not* form a large part of the diet though, as they contain considerable fat, and your pets might develop a waistline problem!

GREENS

Dry food should be supplemented with greens several times weekly to supply additional vitamins and minerals. You can offer fresh lettuce, celery, carrots, kale, parsley, parsnips, apple peel, grass, dandelion, alfalfa, and similar foods in *small* amounts. Your pets are not as susceptible to diarrhea as are some other small rodents. Nevertheless, greens should be given only in *limited* quantities to avoid the risk of intestinal disorders.

Within the limitations discussed, the gerbil's diet allows you considerable possibilities for variation. Individual animals may show certain food preferences, and you'll enjoy testing their tastes from time to time.

With all of the taste-tempting food items that are available for gerbils, there is no need for your pet to have a boring diet. Shown here are regular pelleted food and treats. Photos courtesy Rolf C. Hagen Corp.

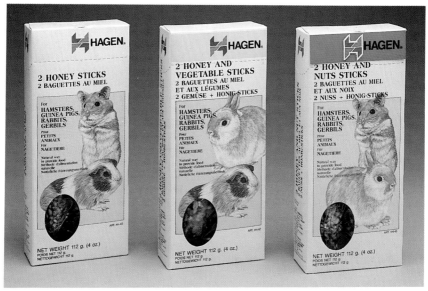

Adding greens to the gerbil's dry-food diet helps furnish necessary vitamins and minerals. Gerbils typically enjoy fresh lettuce, although it doesn't provide as much nourishment as other green vegetables. Photo by Michael Gilroy.

FOOD UTENSILS

Your gerbil's food can be served in a non-tippable, shallow saucer or plate, but an even better alternative is a food hopper that attaches to the side of the cage. Food served in a hopper is less apt to get soiled by droppings and bedding material.

A hanging water bottle is the preferred method of providing water.

WATER

The gerbil's desert heritage means that his drinking water demands are slight; however, fresh water should be available to your pet at all times.

For water purposes, dishes or plates are not satisfactory. The burrowing actions of the animals will upset or contaminate the water. Young gerbils might drown in the container. Additionally, gerbils prefer to drink from a sitting position.

A standard watering bottle costs little, is easily attached to the cage with a spring or wire clip, and helps ensure the water's sanitation. Be sure to choose one with a stainless steel spout. To provide a convenient drinking height, and to prevent the bedding from acting as a wick to drain the bottle, you should locate the bottle so that the end of the spout is several inches above the top of the cage bedding.

If your gerbil cage is an aquarium or other solid-walled container, you can easily bend a length of wire to support the inverted watering bottle inside one corner of the cage.

VACATION TIME

Gerbils travel well, but most likely you'll decide to leave them at home when you go on a vacation. You can leave these pets unattended for several days because of their limited demands.

Before you depart, provide fresh bedding, an accessible container holding plenty of dry food, and a watering bottle of fresh water (make sure it doesn't leak). Give each gerbil a suitably sized chunk of raw carrot; this will supplement their dry diet and provide an "emergency" water supply. Double-check to see that the cage is escape-proof and located where direct sunlight and temperature extremes or drafts will be avoided.

If your vacation is going to be of lengthy duration, of course you must arrange to have someone replenish the animals' food and water *at least* weekly and change the bedding about every two weeks.

Handling

When you first purchase your gerbils, you can offer them food and water, but it's desirable to let them rest for a day before they're handled. This will give them some time to recover from any transportation involved and allow them to become somewhat accustomed to their new home.

HANDLING METHODS

The preferred method of picking up a gerbil is to place one or both hands, cupped with palm up, underneath his body so as to lift him up. At first, let him walk onto your open palm before picking him up; this will prepare him for the experience. Later you can lift him with a gentle, but fairly rapid, scooping motion with one or both hands. Don't grasp his middle—he may feel trapped and struggle to escape.

Once a gerbil is lifted a few inches above any solid surface, he has a good sense of height and will seldom jump or climb down without considerable deliberation.

If you lift your pets to any height, it's a good policy to hold them in the palm of one hand and hold the base of their tail with the other hand to avoid accidental falls. When gerbils are allowed to exercise on a tabletop, they recognize that they should not venture beyond the edge, but in some exuberant moment they might skid off it or simply forget that it's there, and you must be alert to prevent such accidents.

Your pets will enjoy climbing up your arm or your clothes, and they can perch on your shoulder (don't make any abrupt movements that could result in a fall). They like to crawl in and out of collars, pockets, or hoods; be sure that they don't burrow or chew so as to damage your clothing on these occasions.

TAMING AND TRAINING

In thousands of handlings of many different tamed and untamed gerbils of all ages and under varying conditions, the author has never been bitten so that a break in the skin resulted. Several gerbil breeders report similar experiences. Generally a gerbil will bite with force only if he is handled improperly—by chasing, teasing, squeezing, etc. Of course if you place your finger directly in front of his mouth and hold it there, you may receive a slight nip if the animal is hungry or if he's gnawing on some object. This reaction is almost instinctive. If a bite results in broken skin, you should apply appropriate medication and ensure that you are protected against tetanus, as with any other animal bite.

The gerbil's gentleness when handled, his curiosity, friendliness, activity cycle, and food preferences

Neither diurnal nor nocturnal, the gerbil goes through alternating periods of rest and activity throughout the day and night. Generally gerbils are quiet, somewhat timid creatures that are a pleasure to keep. Photo by Michael Gilroy.

Handling the gerbil requires a delicate touch. Never grasp the gerbil's middle, instead allow it to rest on your palm. Eventually the gerbil will grow accustomed to your handling. Photo by Isabelle Francais.

are your clues toward successful taming and training. Also his intelligence seems high for his size. For example, he learns to avoid certain situations or conditions about ten times faster than white rats.

Patience, understanding, repetition, and reward are essential in taming and training. They are your tools for developing in your pets a sense of trust and confidence.

Training sessions should be brief, especially with young gerbils, who may be jumpy and nervous-acting for a few weeks. Keep in mind the gerbil's activity cycle. If you interrupt or prevent a needed rest period, they may become somewhat irritable.

Be slow, calm, and deliberate in your movements and speaking. Let the gerbils become accustomed to your relative size; even your hand may seem like a giant to them!

At feeding time, let the animals eat some seeds or bits of lettuce from your fingers. While they're eating, gently scratch their head, ears, or back with your finger; this will help accustom them to your touch. Later, during training sessions, offer various treats as a reward, especially if you're attempting to teach some simple tricks.

As you progress, let your gerbils out of the cage so that they can have some freedom in a limited area such as a large box, a table top, or even a bathtub. Gerbils will enjoy these outings periodically, especially if you provide some interesting objects to explore. Probably the gerbils will

voluntarily return to their cage for food or rest; otherwise you can easily coax them to return or else pick them up.

You may enjoy staging a gerbil "circus." All you need is a large box, two or more gerbils, some toys and objects that gerbils appreciate, and an appreciative audience. Almost any cardboard or wood box will do, or you can use a metal tub, a plastic sand box, or a rigid wading pool.

Gerbils should not be allowed the run of your household. Eventually they might get lost or injured. However, you might give them the freedom of one room or an enclosed porch occasionally; make sure that the space is sealed off to keep gerbils in and dogs or cats out. You will have to watch your step— literally—because gerbils often come near your feet, either out of curiosity or due to some need for physical security.

Your gerbils can be taken outdoors, weather permitting, but they should be confined to some box, fencing, or other enclosure. If they escape from your control, they could be victims of domestic animals or birds, predators, poisonous sprays, or winter weather.

More easily frightened or nervous gerbils are better not taken outdoors. Likewise, very active and excitable animals may prove too unruly to handle. A good number of gerbil owners advocate a strictly indoor lifestyle for their pets, as an outdoor scenario presents too many unpredictable dangers.

Breeding

In captivity gerbils breed best in mated pairs. Two or more females kept with a single male will result in failure or disaster: either there will be no productive matings or the females may bully the male to death. On losing a mate, a female gerbil is reluctant to receive a new one, and may completely refuse to accept him.

MATURITY AND REPRODUCTION

Sexual maturity occurs between the ages of nine and twelve weeks. Generally the sexes can be distinguished by three weeks. The male's body has a tapered bulge—usually tufted—near the base of his tail, and there is a dark-colored scrotal pouch. The female's rump is more rounded; the genital opening is close to the anal opening. As a rule, mature males are somewhat larger in size and weight than females.

The initial pairing of gerbils nearly always results in compatibility if the pairing is accomplished by maturity. When you buy gerbils from a pet dealer, this detail may already have been taken care of; if not, you'll know in a day or two whether a "happy marriage" will result. Once the pair is thus established, the male can usually be left safely with the female at all times, including during the nursing of a litter.

If desired, you can provide a wood or metal nesting box (with a suitable doorway), but most gerbils seem content with nests built from cloth, paper, or leaves, which they shred into strips with their teeth and forepaws. Both the male and the female participate in this project.

Your pets can breed throughout the year; there is no apparent seasonal variation. Mating often occurs immediately after the arrival of a litter, and sometimes during the nursing period. The gestation period is about 24 days.

Unless you're a careful observer, you may not be able to detect a pregnancy without weighing the female. Because gerbils are naturally so quiet, the first indication of a new litter may be the high-pitched calls of the newborn animals. Most litters are born during the night or early morning; however, the writer has witnessed some births in midafternoon. Birth is relatively uncomplicated and painless, requiring only an hour or so even for a large litter; since there is no help needed on your part, it's advisable that you simply leave the female undisturbed at this time.

The litter size ranges from one to ten, with an average of four or five young; the ratio of males to females is nearly one to one. The majority of females will bear their first litter by age six months. About one-third of all females may have their first litter at age three to four months.

The female's reproductive life may last to age 20 months, although it usually ceases by age 14 months.

SUCCESSFUL BREEDING TIPS

As a pet owner, you may not be able to duplicate some of the favorable conditions achieved by commercial breeders of gerbils. Nevertheless, if you adhere to the following suggestions, you should have an excellent chance of success in breeding your gerbils: 1) Ensure that sufficient cage space, bedding, and nesting material are provided; 2) Keep your gerbils' diet relatively high in protein and low in fat; 3) Provide adequate privacy—a cage with one or more opaque sides may help; 4) Locate the cage where there is a minimum of disturbance from household noise and traffic; 5) Avoid unnecessary handling of your gerbils in the evening.

YOUNG GERBILS

Newborn gerbils are naked and pink, blind, toothless, and deaf. They are little more than an inch long and weigh a tenth of an ounce. The percentage of live births is rather high and cannibalism is rare. If the female should eat her young, it may be that they died from a lack of milk due to some dietary deficiency; you may be able to prevent this by giving the female some evaporated milk during pregnancy and nursing.

The male can be left with the female and the litter, although his "duties" usually consist only of occasional herding the young back to their nest and sitting on the nest to help keep the young warm.

The first week of life is critical. Handling the animals during this period is not recommended—such disturbances might cause the mother to trample, smother, or desert her young unintentionally.

The responsible gerbil parent frequently adjusts the nest bedding to keep the young warm and safe. Photo by Michael Gilroy.

Gerbils are best when kept in mated pairs. These animals are quite prolific when compatible, and are not considered to be monogamous, despite the obvious romantic moment captured here by photographer Michael Gilroy.

Some females fail to raise a small litter successfully, yet their next litter may be a large one in which all young survive. When the young stray from their nest—which can happen at an early age—the mother usually returns them by scooping them with her forefeet, pushing them with her nose, or even by picking them up bodily in her mouth. These measures do not seem to cause any harm. Then she'll busily re-shape the nest to keep all her babies warm and secure. If the litter is large, some females will keep their young in two nests, dividing the nursing time about equally.

Although you can offer some bits of bread crusts soaked in milk, this is not a necessity for a nursing mother if you feed a balanced diet and make drinking water available.

By age three days, the young have some dark pigmentation and they can crawl in an ungainly manner. At five or six days, an undercoat of seal-gray hair is visible and the ears are open. By two weeks the fur is reddish brown. In a few more days, most gerbils have incisors for their first gnawing attempts, their eyelids begin to separate, and their activity is generally more coordinated.

At age three weeks, gerbils weigh about one-half ounce. They can now eat solid food, drink from a watering bottle, climb wire mesh, stand up, jump, and thump their hind legs. Though tiny, they are truly gerbils and they should be weaned now.

This may seem to be a tender age for weaning, but the animals adjust easily, and it is important to remove them from their parents to avoid the space and parental care problems if another litter should arrive in a few days (this is the exception not the rule).

Weanlings may be sexed and placed in separate cages or kept in a community group until they are about eight weeks of age, when they should be separated to prevent inbreeding. In pairing gerbils, it is a good policy to keep their relationship no closer than second cousin.

The young can be housed in smaller quarters than adults, but you should allow about 20 square inches per animal.

For the first week after weaning, you may want to put some unsweetened breakfast cereal in with the gerbils' regular solid food; this is easily handled and the animals seem to like it. Some milk-soaked bread crusts may be offered also, if desired. The use of a watering bottle is quickly learned if the spout is positioned so that the young can reach it.

Some litters may have one or two runts, due to nursing difficulties or dietary deficiencies. Often these gerbils will grow to normal size and catch up with others of their litter. If the runts are bullied by their brothers and sisters, you can isolate the runts to permit an opportunity for more unhindered development.

Health

The gerbil is relatively healthy and hardy and will remain so

with a minimum of care from their owner. You can expect their normal life span to be three to five years.

Preventive measures are important because the successful treatment of some diseases of small animals is difficult to impossible. Preventive measures include proper diet, fresh water, reasonable cleanliness, sufficient cage space and ventilation, and protection against dampness and extreme temperatures or drafts.

Diarrhea and other intestinal disorders seem to be rare among gerbils. If such illnesses occur, they could be related to the diet—perhaps too many leafy greens, or the presence of contaminated food.

Colds and similar conditions are seldom a problem but their symptoms include listless activity or droopiness, runny eyes or nose, and lack of appetite.

Balding, eye injuries, body sores and external parasites may sometimes affect the gerbil. Always consult your veterinarian first.

Bibliography

GERBILS
By Paul Paradise
ISBN 0-87666-927-5
KW-037
Audience: The gerbil keeper and admirer looking for specific information on the proper care of the animal. Like all other members of this handy series, this book offers sensible and accessible recommendations to the fancier.
Hardcover, 5½ x 8", completely illustrated with full-color photos and drawings. 96 pages.

GERBILS: A Complete Introduction
By Mrs. M. Ostrow
ISBN 0-86622-267-7
CO-018
Audience: All of the basics of good care, management and breeding presented in tandem with colorful photos of this playful little rodent. Different color varieties captured in photographs. All books in this series strive to bring the beginner a complete and useful approach to animal husbandry.
Hardcover, 5½ x 8 ½", full-color photos, plus helpful line drawings. 128 pages.

PROFESSIONAL'S BOOK OF GERBILS
By Bob Bernhard
ISBN 0-86622-669-9
H-909
Audience: Beyond an introductory text, this comprehensive book is refreshingly complete and well written. The author concentrates on providing information that readers will be able to put to good use and benefit from; the beginner and the experienced gerbil keeper will surely deem this an indispensable companion to gerbil care and breeding.
Hardcover, 5½ x 8½", 75 full-color photos. 160 pages.